# With a Thankful Heart

Betty Swink Martin

D1521354

Dedicated to the Glory of God

*"He has turned my wailing into dancing, removed my sackcloth, and clothed me with joy that my heart may sing to Him and not be silent. O Lord, my God, I will give you thanks forever."*

*Psalm 30:11-12*

# CONTENTS

These conversations, stories and prayers were begun when as a young wife and mother I attended a Christian prayer retreat. At some point during this renewal weekend, we were asked to find a quiet spot, take pen and pencil, and write a letter to God. We were instructed to wait patiently after completing this, then begin to write. God spoke to my spirit that day as I wrote His words in answer to my prayer. It is true. God does speak to His children in many ways. And this is one of them.

I have come to realize that God wants these prayers, thoughts, conversations, and stories assembled. The words are not mine. God has given them to me during specific times of quiet or when I have been truly crying out to Him. It is my fervent prayer that God through Jesus Christ, in the power of the Holy Spirit, will use this text to open your eyes to the reality of God as your loving caring Father. Your Father, who really does speak to you, and who really does answer your prayers.

In His love,
Betty Swink Martin
January 17, 1994

## By Unseen Chains

Dear Father.
I love you God!
I am free through your grace in Christ Jesus.
Bound not by unseen chains!
My Lord,
Thank you for freeing me!
Thank you for your relaxing exhilarating presence in my life!
The healthy joy of being your child, given new life.
My Father! My Father!
How I worship you.
You have taken me as I was,
and through Jesus Christ, you have made a new person.
Dear, Dear God!
Thank you for Jesus,
The Miracle in my life!

# Finally Home

*Luke 15:11-32 & Luke 23:34*

It was a cold snowy Christmas Eve, and in the distance the old man could see the twinkling of lights in the store windows. It was late, and the people he had heard earlier in the evening had left the street deserted but for him. In the quiet of the night be remembered a once upon a time home, a loving wife, and a young son, but the quickly stabbing pain of yesterday hurt too deeply.

He shook the memories away, huddled against a building, and pulled his tattered coat tightly about his neck. The wind was bitingly cold as it swept through his body. The snow swirled menacingly around him threatening to overpower him in the black winter night and he was its willing victim.

He knew where to find sanctuary. He knew the escape route. It was just up the street and around the corner. There was a small church open for people like him. He had been there last night. He had heard carols being sung, and he ventured inside. Someone had come to him, offered a meal, and then provided a bed for the night. And someone had prayed for him. But he couldn't go back.

As he waited for the sleep, he sought to overtake him, he reflected on the life he had lived. Many years ago, as a young father he had turned away from his family, leaving his wife and son. Doing what he wanted to do going where he wanted to go, his life sped by. He knew how selfish he had been and what he had become. He had walked in his own unforgiveness these last years of his life. He was an alcoholic with nothing and no one. He had shuffled along from town to town, odd job to odd job until he couldn't go any more.

He found himself here in his hometown. He knew the church, the sanctuary. He remembered it well. He had married in that church up the street and around the corner. And it was there he had gone last night. He really didn't know why. Maybe he was looking for the yesterdays he had so freely given away.

He hadn't expected to find the church open, but he heard the music and entered the church hesitantly. He had been accepted with no questions asked, fed, and given a warm bed. He had awakened during the night to find the man who had fed him kneeling beside him, and the old man, so tired, so deeply worn. listened as the stranger prayed. The man's soothing voice lulled him to sleep again.

He awoke the next morning, shaking with the symptoms of the addiction that had overcome him, and slowly took in his surroundings. He looked across the room and saw the same man who had prayed for him helping to feed the hungry as they filled the small eating area in the back of the room.

The man looked up, saw the elderly man struggling to his feet. and hurried over to help him. He had the gentleness of a shepherd holding a dying lamb in his arms as he reached out to offer his strength to this pathetic old man. Placing his arm around the older man's shoulders, he explained that he was the minister of the small church, and then he told the old man his name.

When he heard the minister's name, the weather-hardened wrinkled face broke and years of unshed tears ran like rivers and fell onto the hands of the man who so tenderly held him. The old man moved away, saying nothing. He left the church and wandered aimlessly down the sidewalk.

And here he was now, in the midnight of his life. He had made up his mind. The cold would finally cause the numbness to begin, and he would go quietly to sleep. The snow would cover him, and all the pain, failures, and loneliness would be over. If the cold would just do its job faster.

Then he heard the voice of the man from the church, the man who had fed him, held him. and prayed for him. He felt himself being wrapped in the warmth of a blanket and lifted in the minister's strong arms. The voice, the arms, of the son he had deserted so many years ago.

The old man heard, "Where have you been? I've looked and looked for you for such a very, very long time." With these words the old man looked into his son's gentle loving eyes and then slumped on his shoulder. His son shifted his father's weight, pulled him close, and quietly said, "Come on, Dad. Let's go home."

The old man, out of darkness and enveloped in the light of love, was finally home, once more a Christmas gift wrapped in a rough woolen blanket and tied in his son's forgiving arms, received with a grateful heart...

*The people that walked in darkness have seen a great Light:*
*They that dwell in the land of the shadow of death, upon them hath the Light shined.*
*Isaiah 9:2 (KJV)*

The Son of God, Jesus the Christ,
The Light of the world came, lived His life on this earth, and as He was dying,
He said, "Father, Forgive them. They don't know what they are doing."
We are to do no less.
It is in the forgiving of yesterday's hurts, forgiving of ourselves and of others,
we find the sweetness of who Jesus really is.
He lifts us in His strong arms and carries us out of the darkness into His complete Light.
Jesus Christ, our Savior.

# All the Light in the World

*Luke 11:36*

The little girl found a corner in the darkness of her room, wedged herself in, and looked out into the blackness of the night with large watchful eyes.

"Where is Mama?" She wondered.

Her mother had put her to sleep only a few hours earlier singing sweet songs of love into her little ears. She had awakened to find herself alone in her room... in her room where there was no light.

She didn't like the dark. The little girl had tried to leave her room to find her mother, but nighttime was very scary, and the house was so big. Finally, she had given up and sought safety in a wee corner near her bed. She listened to the strange noises just outside her window. Her once cozy room seemed to be filled with creaks and groans and night sounds. Tears began to run down her cheeks as she clutched her worn blanket in her little fists and buried her face in its soft folds.

Then... in the distance she could hear the softest of tippy-toeing footsteps. She raised her head and saw the faint glow of candlelight. The light grew stronger, and miracle of miracles, her mother appeared in the doorway. Her beautiful face was bathed in glowing wonderful light.

"Oh, my darling, " Mama quietly said. "There is no reason to fear. Even when there appears to be no light, the candle is always nearby. And Mother is always, always here."

She ran to her mother, threw her arms around her neck, and was gently lifted into loving arms. Her mother placed the candle in the candlestick near the window, and she and her little girl lay down. The little girl settled into her special place, the nook within her mama's arms, looked up into her mother's eyes, and saw the light from the candle reflected in them. Her mama... all the light in the world to this baby girl. Her eyelashes dusted her cheeks, and soon she was sleeping the night away in childlike trust and peace.

I have been this baby girl. I have found myself in what appeared to be dark places. I have cried out, and the Candle of the Lord, Jesus the Christ, came, shining away the darkness and, always in all ways, making everything full of His incredibly wonderful light. Sometimes He comes as a still small voice. Always I find Him in His Word, and I also see His light in you.

My prayer for you is that Jesus, the Light of the World, would shine so beautifully for you and in you, that others will see His light in your own brightly lit candle, find His comfort, and receive Him so that they too may rest in His light, because Jesus is always, always here... right here in each one of us.

## The Light

Jesus, the Light in my Life.
When I walk in the light, I forget how bad the darkness is.
The light removes the darkness,
And I know the total reality of God and His Word.
I have sometimes slowly slipped away from the light.
The door to my spirit isn't wide open.
I don't sit at the feet of Jesus and rest.
I haven't eaten from the Bread of Life
or drunk the new wine of Jesus Christ.
And the darkness tries to enter again.
But Jesus stays with me.
He knocks and knocks because I am His.
The door to my spirit begins to widen.
He begins to feed me the sustenance of His bread.
I sup from His cup and become filled with His fruit.
I throw open the door with absolute trust,
And I am wholly in His light, again.
The light...that wonderful, marvelous ever enveloping light.

Lord,
The day is so bright
Your way is right
Help us to stay close in your light

## Trust

His mother had told her three-year-old son that Jesus lived in him...and the little boy thought really hard about this.

One night he had a bad dream and woke up crying for his mama. The next night as his mother was putting him to bed she prayed, "Dear God, take care of my precious little boy, and please don't let him have any bad dreams or be afraid during the night."

The small boy, listening closely to this prayer, remembered Mama had said that Jesus lived in him, so he pulled up the top of his pajamas and said, "Tell Jesus too, Mama."

That's what trust is... Trust in Mama to ask Jesus to make it all right and knowing that she would, and He would...It's just that easy...

## Lord, Today I Saw a Hungry Child

Today I saw a hungry child.
He didn't quite fit the mold.
He hungered for acceptance.
I gave him no place in my life.
He lingered near me.
He hungered for a touch.
I chose to turn away.
He hungered for a kind word.
I didn't have the time.
He hungered for understanding.
I didn't want to try.
He really hungered for love.
I could give him none.
Then You said,
"Don't pass him by... Don't go to the other side."
Today, I saw a hungry child.
He didn't quite fit the mold.
He hungered for acceptance.
You gave him a place in my life.
He lingered near me.
He hungered for a touch.
You gave him my hand.
He hungered for a kind word.
You gave me words of encouragement just for him.
He hungered for understanding.
You gave me your wisdom as I looked into his heart.
He really hungered for love.
You gave him You in me.

Jesus said, "Suffer the little children to come unto me for such is the kingdom of God."

God's children... all shapes... all sizes... all needing all kinds of things. I don't want to pass one of your children by, Lord, and I don't want to be passed by either. Because, Father, sometimes I'm one of those hungry children.

# Daddy, Look at My Heart

Her mother works sixty-hour weeks, and her father is an addict living in a world where children don't belong. This wisp of a child has witnessed and heard the worst of the world. Her daddy's addiction caused the loss of her home and the breakup of her family. She has seen her mother cry in desperation and weariness. Her dad doesn't provide for this daughter. He loves her, but he has lost understanding of her neediness. The need isn't just for food, clothing, and shelter. She needs her daddy, but her daddy doesn't (can't) understand, and she doesn't (can't) understand.

Oh, Lord, how fragile are our children.

Her mother, sister, and grandparents provide the stability in her life. Her mom and grandparents take her to church, and she listens quietly as she learns about her Father, God, and His Son, Jesus.

She had innocence in her face when one Sunday the pastor asked the children of the church, "Would you like to ask Jesus to come into your heart?" She shyly raised her small hand, and there that day Jesus became a part of her. That afternoon turning her shining face and looking into her grandmother's eyes, she pulled up her little shirt and asked, "Do you see Jesus in my heart?"

Throughout her young life she has quietly watched the lifestyle of her earthly father—she loves him so very much...but through the dedication of a Christian mother and Godly grandparents she has, at the age of five, chosen the better way, the only way to her Father God, Jesus the Christ. It may be that one day her dad will see in her heart this Jesus, and he, too, will find this better way.

The purity, the innocence, the trust, the miracle of a little child. Thank you, God, for giving us children. Forgive us when we fail them. Thank you that you never do.

# One Day... Understanding

The daughter turned away as the doctor began to speak. These were words she really didn't want to hear. She walked from the waiting room, turned the corner, and leaned her head against the wall. The pain was inexpressible. Mama...

Three years later she would find herself in a room in a nursing home, looking at her mother as she lay wracked with pain. The daughter heard the sounds of suffering. And finally, she gave her mother up, heard her mother breathe her last breath, and watched her beloved mother die.

She had fought hard for her mother's life. Reaching out to the only possible answer...God Himself. She had so desperately sought a miracle, but the healing she had expected did not come. She didn't understand...

Her mother hadn't wanted to leave her home, and she shouldn't have had to do so. Her mother shouldn't have died in a nursing home. She had been an ideal mother. She had loved her children and lived her life around them. She was the mom who always had a pie or cake ready when her children walked through the door. The mom who ironed, cooked, laughed, starched petticoats, and sat up waiting... A mother who was always there. The kind of mom who deserves more than a nursing home the last three months of her life.

The family tried to keep her at home, but that last trip to the hospital had brought the realization that their mom had to have constant care. Her brother lived in Florida. Her sister lived in Texas and was pregnant. She had lost her first child in delivery, and all care was being taken to insure a healthy mother and baby. And this daughter lived in Tennessee. All three were so far away from the hometown of their youth.

The adult children's parents needed them, and, in reality, they had done everything they could. They were young and had little finances to help provide care for their mother in the childhood home. Their eighty-four-year-old father had managed for a while with daytime help, but it became evident this wasn't enough. It was a tremendously difficult decision.

It would take years before she could forgive herself...even though she knew there wasn't another way.

Several weeks after her mother had died the daughter had a dream. Her mother was walking along the top of an earthen dam. She was not dressed, but she was walking away, and her back was covered with the long, wavy, beautiful, black hair of her youth. Her body was healthy and so like the daughter remembered when her mama was well. It was obvious her mother was happy. Seconds after she was walking along the dam, she was under the water held back by the dam. Above the place where she entered the water were bubbles carrying these words: "Rivers of life, rivers of life, rivers of life..." She knew God had given her a vision of her mother alive forever with Him.

It has been eighteen years. This daughter misses her mother, and she will probably always cry when she hears, "Tell me the story of Jesus... Write on my heart every word..." It was a chorus her mother sang.

She had loved her mother, loves her still, profoundly, but she knows she will see her again, and her mama will be beautiful and happy just as she was in the dream...then the daughter will understand why.

*For now we see through a glass darkly, but then face to face.*
*I Corinthians 13:12a*

## Today I'm Just a Plain Ordinary Sparrow

I've prayed and sought the Lord. I've read my Bible and studied His word. I get to going in the right direction for a while, then somehow, I always slip. It's like there is this big classroom, and all of us are in it together. There are the excellent students who seem born to understand, to have the visitations from the angels, and to feel the warm oil of the Holy Spirit flowing over them. They just have it altogether. They're the soaring eagles. I listen to their testimonies of what they have actually seen and heard. I hear them sing anointed songs with anointed voices, and I hear them speak of miracles just like I read in God's Word and there I am in the midst of all these eagles... a sparrow.

You know, I believe God's Word, too. I made up my mind several years ago that all the Bible is truth. God's truth. I know Jesus is real—that He saves, heals, delivers, anoints, and, well, basically, He does all things 100 percent right. So...

I'm really glad God said he cares about the sparrows and the lilies of the field because more and more I have come to realize I'm just a plain ordinary person. Oh, don't misunderstand. I know God has given gifts to all his children and He has given me mine. It's just that sometimes for me, they're so very hard to find. When I read of the miracles of yesterday and hear of those today, my faith begins to climb. I know it's real...He says it's real.

Today in this gigantic classroom here on Earth I am an ordinary student. And that's okay. One day God will have His way and make me into one with better than average passing grades to get past the sparrow status, because I really would like to be an eagle.

God knows it's a whole lot easier than we think. It's just a matter of trust. I do believe He has so much more for us if we will rest our lives in Him, commune with Him, and believe what He says. In order to do that, we have to listen to Him, talk with Him, and read His Word. We have to do our homework. I've got to get my mind to listen to my spirit.

Do your homework... Do your homework... Do it every day. The eagle is waiting to take flight...

In the meantime, Lord, thanks for loving the eagles and the sparrows all the same.

Dear Father,

I love you, God!
I am free through your grace in Christ Jesus.
Bound not by unseen chains!

My Lord,
Thank you for freeing me!
Thank you for your relaxing, exhilarating presence in my life!
The healthy joy of being your child, given new life.

My Father! My Father!
How I worship you.
You have taken me as I was.
And through Jesus Christ, you have made a new person.

Dear, Dear God!
Thank you for Jesus, The Miracle in my life!

## Today

Today I renew my mind in the Word of God.
I fight the good fight of faith.
Forgetting the sins of my humanness
as my Father,
through the blood of Jesus Christ,
washes me clean again.
I walk in the counsel of the Word of God.
My Father is constantly with me!

I trust God
as my Father, my creator, my friend, and my strength.
I am a child of the living God.
I walk in Jesus Christ.
Jesus is my Savior
The light of Jesus is shining in me.

I trust Jesus
as my intercessor, my friend, my deliverer, and my healer.
The Holy Spirit lives in me.

I trust the Holy Spirit
to fill me completely with His presence as my comforter and the source of
faithfulness, gentleness, goodness, joy, kindness, love, patience, peace, and
self-control,
fruit of the Spirit of God in my life.

I trust the Father, Son, and Holy Spirit to be 100% in control of my life.
I am freed, forgiven, and freshly alive!

# New Life

She stood at the picture window looking at the first green blades of the spring daffodils. She loved the beauty of the flower garden, and always before she had waited with excited anticipation for this time of year. She would scratch in the earth, disregarding the broken fingernails and soiled hands. Her search was enchanting to her as she looked for the tiny, furled fronds of the fern and the heart shaped leaves of the wild violet. Always the flower garden had been a therapy for her. Planting, watering, weeding, and sharing the abundance of beauty caused sunshine in her life.

She was forty. She thought about that as she visited with her friends, the daffodils. Her son, her only child, was eighteen now and was looking forward to college in the fall. The freedom from parental authority and the fun-filled days of collegiate life were mesmerizing to him. She would miss him for he was her blessing from God. He was so loved. She knew she loved too deeply, too emotionally. When he thinks of his mother as he grows older, will he remember her wet, dirty, and smiling in her flower bed? She hoped he would.

She had been married for almost twenty years. They had met in college. He had been so good to her, and she fell in love with that. They married six months after they met, and their son was born a year and a half later. He held them together through the years like the soft moist earth holds the daffodil bulbs now. The bulbs grow larger and produce more and more. There was quite a family there in the soil outside her window. She had not been like the fertile bulbs. Her son was all the children in the world to her and her husband. Their love covered him and each other just as the autumn leaves protect the tender young plants in her spring garden.

Her son was leaving in September. She had known that. Now her husband had left. Their marriage had survived many crises, financial reversal, job transfers, and the deaths of their parents. They had talked of divorce, but she could never imagine her life without him. They had always known that she was his, and he was hers. God had given them to each other to be one flesh. To comfort one another in the midst of life's trials and rejoice together in life's joys.

It had been a hard winter. The plants in her garden needed care. Many tender branches killed by the freezing temperatures needed to be cut away from the healthy plants. The plants would produce many new branches due to the pruning she would do. She felt like part of her had also been cut out, that a very major part of her emotional and physical body was gone. All of her that remained cried, even when there were no tears, she cried. She was so tired...so very tired.

Through the intensity of the pain, she knew that she had played a part in this decision her husband had made. It was a time for growing up and she was ready to do this. She remembered when her husband pruned a newly planted oak tree. How she had fussed, but he had assured her that the mature tree would be beautifully shaped. And it was. Now, it was time to take a penetrating look at herself, to allow God to reshape her. She would learn through this reality. To let the pain teach her.

After the daffodils bloom, the green blades of foliage must be left to slowly fade and eventually die. They were such a contrast to the golden flowers that once filled everything within their view with sunlight. She was always tempted to trim them neatly back to the ground, but the experience she had as a gardener told her to wait. The energy for the blooms for the next season were in those dying leaves. That's what she would have to do now. She would have to wait.

She was willing to let God show her to herself. To look at who she really was. God could take the woman she was, heal the hurts, and help her make the changes she needed to make. And from the old, she would learn. Only He could renew her and fill her with His abundant light-filled energy. To remind her of who she is in Christ Jesus.

She made a decision as she leaned against the window. She chose to remember that God had brought her husband and her together and blessed them with a son. She chose to believe for a miracle, the healing of her marriage, the healing of her family.

There would be scars. But she also understood that when the healing is complete, the scarred tissue is the strongest. When she recalls the scars, she'll remember the one that taught her how deeply she loves her husband, the scar that grew her up, and the scar that reminds her that with every breath she believes in her family.

She knew what she believed. She believed in God, the realities of life, and the survival of home, family, love, honor, and devotion. Tough times come, and tough times go. The storms of life are a part of reality. Just as storms of nature pass and peace descends, so it is in life. She understood what a storm could do in her garden and in her family. But those daffodil bulbs...they were always safe and always growing. That's the way her family had been and would be again safe, growing, and loving.

Postscript: The children are coming home tomorrow. The children: Their son, his wife, and two children—a grandson and a granddaughter. It's Thanksgiving, and her husband is cooking the turkey and all the trimmings. Her family—safe, growing, and loving...blessed of God.

16

## A Heart at Peace Gives Life to the Body

*Proverbs 14:30*

There was a time in my life when I sought lasting peace but could not find it.
My days and nights were darkness. I longed for a quiet place,
where God's peace could grow and become a part of me.
A place that would fill me with His light far from the darkness.

I needed time.
Time to place my feet in a stream of gently running water.
Far away from the world of man.
Time to listen. Yes, listen, listen to the quiet.
Time to hear the song of the bird once again, and watch the wind run
through the trees.
Time to choose my place to sit, to rest, to meditate on my Father's creative
power.

As I sped through this earthly life, I cried out!
And God heard my cries.
He reached down and caused me to be still.
He reminded me that He is my Good Shepherd.
He led me to that still water, and He gave me His peace.
I placed my heart at His feet, and I went forward into His rest.

His light had broken through the darkness.
He filled me with the glory of His truth.
My feet were planted in the Living Water of His Word.
As I supped freely from His Living Bread, He reminded me that it is good to
sit with Him and rest beside Him.

God is the quiet, but I heard Him in the running water, in the song of the
bird, and as He walked on the wings of the wind.
I arose recreated—God truly had redeemed me.
His peace penetrated my soul, my body, and my spirit.
He has called me to enter the world of man again.
This time I walk with God in His stillness.
His peace dwells within me and I'll never be in darkness again.

## Peace

I call you into my rest, and I want you to remember that your peace is my peace. There isn't any peace in the world. I meant for there to be an Earth filled with my love, for in my love is the perfect peace that the world is seeking. But men follow their own dreams and listen little to me. The calling of the world is an entrapment, and many called...fall, and my voice gets hidden from them as they rush about listening to others rather than to me. Many have cried out to me in their snares, and I have grabbed them and held them close to me, for these heard my voice and answered me.

## Listen

Listen with the ear of your spirit.
"Seek me, seek me with your whole heart."
Hear Him as He asks,
"Is the world's daily news so much more important than mine?"
Listen,
Hear Him,
"Come Let's talk awhile before you enter the busyness of the day."
Listen,
Do you hear Him?
"Is the television program more interesting than me?
It's not that I don't want you to enjoy this life I've given you,
But don't you remember?
I came to give you life, and to give it to you more abundantly.
Listen
You need me.
I am that abundant life.
I want to give you so much more than what fills your life today.
I'm very close to you.
Are you very close to me?
Remember, you must seek me diligently with your whole heart."
Listen,
Did you hear Him when He called you today?

### Listen, Hear My Voice

The way I have chosen for you has taught you many important truths. Let me continue to teach you. Today is the day I have made.

Today. You have the grace to live today. Not yesterday and not tomorrow. Today, serve me. Today, be as Jesus is. You must allow Me, through Jesus and the Holy Spirit, to mold you after My will. My ears listen for and to your cry. Let Me respond to you by making you truly free, for I came to set the captives free. You are a free child in Christ.

You are hiding inside. Come out. Bring the Sonshine out. Remember, be careful for nothing. You are being taken care of. Rest and know that I am your God. When you rest in Jesus, then My light will shine fully in you. Sit back and relax in My care. Love...Love...Love...and only by My grace, through the blood of Jesus Christ, My Son, and by My Holy Spirit is this possible. Slow down and live.

## In His Stillness

I hear the sweet flowing of a spring fed river,
the calming sound of running water.
singing quiet praise to the Maker.
I see the cool clearness of its waters.
and rocks washed smooth by centuries of current.
The trees bend near the river's banks.
with leaves caressing the tranquil stream.

I enter and find a quiet spot resting in God's beauty.
The soft wind blows gentle kisses against my face.
The colors of nature surround me,
miracles of blues and greens and browns.
I Praise God who has given these remote places,
places of solitude and reflection His perfect peace.

*And He leads me beside the still waters.*
*Psalm 23*

## Silence

I would ask of thee, my Father, "What is silence?"
Silence is the complete overwhelmingness of My presence in you... in which
you rest so in Me...that in your silence I AM!

The silence of Your Presence, Father, brings the refreshing Holy Spirit
anointing me to Your service this day to do your good will and pleasure,
inviting me to accompany You as You make every moment in my life
beneficial to others and to me as you walk, talk, and live in me accomplishing
in Your Presence Your perfection for the day.

Lord,

This is quiet day. I'm the only person in my home. and there isn't any noise.
Even the dog is resting somewhere other than at my feet. Quiet, today, is
good. I enjoyed the lingering bath with the two small candles lit. Somehow
the flickering soft light is calming. The music of praise spilled into my quiet
time as I listened to beautiful songs sung glorying you. This old chenille
bathroom is comfortable. And my wet hair a sign of unhurried bliss. You see,
I don't have to be anywhere today...This is so good! Thank you for this
freedom, to relax, to work a crossword puzzle, to pop some real popcorn,
prop up on several pillows, cover up with a worn treasured quilt, and watch a
wonderful lighthearted old movie. Wow! Lord, I really needed this day. Thank
you for bringing it into my life and thank you for giving me the wisdom to
take it, to rest. I'm having such a good time with you. Why? Oh, why don't I
rest with you more often?

## These Our Friends

*Ointment and perfume rejoice the heart: so does the sweetness of a man's friend by hearty counsel.*
*Proverbs 27:9*

Friendships are built in the realities of life and in the sharing of experiences. I've never had a quickly formed friendship that lasted. Quick friendships are like the annuals in my garden. They bloom and are beautiful for a season. Then with the first frost they begin to dry up and die.

Friends don't have to believe the same way, act the same way, or live the same way. But we do have to trust the same way. And we do have to give so very much of ourselves.

We must be willing to take what our friend offers us—love, help, and understanding. We must give the same. It is the continuous giving and taking that form the crucible of deeply rooted life-long friendships.

Many people join us in walking through the myriads of life's joys, but few will crawl through the valleys with us. Listening to our heartache and reassuring us there is a mountain top after the valley. When the facade we wear breaks, and the pain is evident, those who are willing to share it bear the mark of friendship.

We see Godly strength and human weakness and we accept both. We share tears of grief together. We comfort the broken hearted and we are comforted. And we laugh together—we laugh a lot.

## A Prayer for a Friend

Dear God,

My friend is so very sick. She has the only hope there is—your control in her life. Lord, through the tears, please ever be her constant companion. Please, Lord, apply the Blood of Jesus to her body. Be in total control. Take over, Father. Breathe on her, Holy Spirit. Give her the breath of your living life. Lord, man has said horrifying words, but your words are life and health to her flesh. Oh, God, replace her blood with the pure spotless blood of Jesus the Christ. Her Savior, her deliver, her healer... Lord, just today I gave you total control. I did this because I trust in you and your word. God, don't let anything or anyone come between my friend and your perfect will for her life. Today, Father, be in that room. Jesus visit her. Live in her. Fill her. I believe you, Lord. Keep her under the shelter of your wings. Give her your complete and perfect rest, Lord. Cause the fear to depart. Rebuke it, Jesus. For God, this is a battle you have already won at Jesus' cross, grave, and resurrection.

In Jesus.

*Then came the word of the Lord unto Jeremiah saying, behold, I am the Lord, the God of all flesh. Is there anything too hard for me?*
*Jeremiah 32:26-27*

## We Need to Talk, Lord

This is a very heavy burden and...here I am again, Lord...the place where I thought I'd never be again. On the bottom. If I would just make the effort to get up. Sometimes, I just get tired of trying so hard to do the right thing, to say the right thing, and to act the right way. I don't want to be out of your will, but you know this burden I'm carrying has me weighed down. Even though in my spirit, I know everything is perfectly alright.

Is there anybody else in your kingdom like me? Probably not. You made us all different, didn't you, Lord? Why is it so hard for me to stay comfortably peaceful and full of your joy? I know being in your peace and joy is the very best place to be. I feel so full of guilt, and I get angry with myself when I act like this. By now, I should have living this life in Christ down pat, but the simple truth is you are going to have to get me through this.

I could put it in lots of lovely churchy phrases, but I can't do anything without you so help, just plain help me give you this burden and let your peace and joy return to me.

Oh, God, help me... I'm so tired of trying so hard...

Picture yourself in my arms just like the infant, Katie, lying in the arms of her mother. Did you see the unlined, smooth, lovely face of the peaceful child? She rests in the arms of love, perfectly nourished and clothed as a chosen child. She is touched by tender hands that minister to her every need. Eyes are open to her slightest movement, and attentive ears listen to every sound she utters. She is an adored, blessed, precious child, cared for with wisdom and absolute devotion. If these earthly parents love so deeply, my child, how much more am I able to love and sustain you?

Rest in me...Come unto me all ye who are heavy burdened, and I will give you rest.

An Answered Prayer
The doctor had said there might be a problem, but...
On July 26, 1994, Hayley Elizabeth Martin was born to Michael Alton and Tracy Elizabeth Martin.
She is perfectly formed by her Father God, beautiful in every way.
May the grace of Almighty God always in all ways rest upon her.

### The Sun is Shining, Lord!

Lord, it was ten o'clock when I turned over in bed this wonderful Saturday morning. The sun is shining so brightly through the windows that I have thrown open the doors, pulled the blinds to the tops of the windows, and pushed the curtains over as far as they will go on the rods.

The sun is shining! It's the middle of April, and I cherish the blue sky, the hanging bridal wreath laden with blossoms as white as the dress of the virgin bride, and the fragrant purple phlox filling the air with nature's own perfume.

I love the bees hovering over individual flowers. It is the middle of their workday. But here I am just beginning mine. Lord, I am so grateful to you for this incomparable day. A new day. A day filled with hope, completely pressureless. Thank you for the luxury of sleeping late, this freshly brewed, special cup of hazelnut coffee, and this time with you.

Father, I just want to tell you how wonderful it is not to be rushed. This is so special. You try so hard to tell me to relax and now here is this fantastic day you have placed before me. And you know what, Lord, I'm going to play today!

There's the still cool earth there in my garden waiting for me to begin my day of digging, pulling weeds, and planting. What a treasured time! I want to make that new flower bed in the backyard.

God, I'm so thankful to you for this day. Surround me with your presence as the birds make their nests and search for food, the butterflies drift on the light currents of sunlit air, and my dog follows me about my work. Continue to remind me of the pleasure of this glorious day.

Walk with me, God, talk with me in my garden. You made the garden. You meant it to be perfect and in Jesus the Christ it now can be perfect again. So, let's go forward into this day of Sonlight... this sun filled April day.

## Were You Still With Me?

Yes, Lord. It was a Beautiful Day. But didn't I mess it up…?

Didn't everything just start out great, Father? The sun shining, the birds singing, and there I was fairly lapping it up and talking with you! What a beginning! I even invited you along to walk with me in this glorious day in my garden.

So, I dressed for my yard work. Since I am well past the age of wanting a suntan and into the age of avoiding sunspots, I smeared my face up quite well with number 15 sunscreen and skin conditioner, pulled on my old faded green jeans, buttoned up the torn, rather ratty, blue flannel shirt, and laced up my favorite, ready for the trash, tennis shoes. Then I put on my white baseball cap, which carries an advertisement for a weed killer of some kind, and the finishing touch was my new pair of green and yellow garden gloves. Well, You were there. You know what I looked like. I was ready to tackle my backyard and stay in it.

Out the door my, friendly as a Pitbull, Schnauzer, Nick, You, and I went ready for the job of shaping the yard into spring beauty. Looking around, I realized before I could really get down to having the real fun of planting the shrubs and flowers, there was some basic work that had to be done. I grabbed my, what I considered, new rake and began the task of removing the signs of fall that still remained clinging to my yard.

That's when it happened, Lord. Granted the rake was about six weeks old and had been used TWICE for prior leaf raking projects, but did it have to fall apart THIS SATURDAY?

So, what did I do? Did I react like any normal Christian, middle aged, fairly intelligent, wife, mother, sister, mother-in-law, teacher, and grandmother? Did I happen to remind myself of our wonderful visit in the a.m.? Not me! My great Saturday morning attitude fell apart.

I basically began a silent tirade about the inferiority of the goods I purchase, and didn't these people know they were messing around with my time, my money, and my SATURDAY?

Were You still with me here, Lord?

There I was standing the yard, looking at what was once my new shiny blue rake, then, practically before I knew it, the rake and I were in my car headed back to the rake's original home. And I was in the parking lot in my Saturday finery—faded jeans, torn shirt buttoned to the neck, worn out tennis shoes, baseball cap with the weed killer advertisement, NEW green and yellow gloves, and an oily sun screened face.

I made a quick decision—I was NOT going to walk from the return counter all the way to the garden center and back again. People would see me!

So, the parts of the rake and I boldly entered the garden center and went directly to the checkout counter. As I stood in line, withstanding a few double takes, I vaguely remembered that the pair of jeans I had on might be the ones with all the holes across the rear.

Were you still with me here, Lord?

Someone suggested that a teenage boy standing in the garden area MIGHT be able to help me. This was a wrong move. Of course, he couldn't replace my rake. I had to go to the return counter. Return counter? Not this lady! I told him and I told him. He suggested I talk to the manager. Good idea!

You heard me... didn't you, Lord?

As I was impatiently leaning on boxes of garden implements two people approached me—a lady, who wanted to know how much the petunias were, and a man, the manager, who didn't know why he was there. I was beginning to calm down, so I explained my situation in a rational manner. He shook his head because, obviously, he had been called from more important jobs to handle my problem. But he returned my old rake and brought me a new one. I did get my way.

You were shaking your head, too. Weren't you. Lord?

As I drove home, I was still mulling over American economics.

*All it would have taken to solve the problem was to attach the head of the rake to the handle with a single nail or screw. There was already a hole drilled in the rake. Why wasn't there a nail? I just ought to write the CEO of this major American corporation and let him know what I think.*

But the rake wasn't the problem was it, Father? The problem was that my patience was tested, and I failed. My pride was tested, and it failed. It wasn't just the rake that fell apart, was it, Lord? And you were there weren't you, Father? But I didn't ask you to help me, did I?

After all that, we still had a great day. because even when I mess things up, you are always there to help me straighten them out again. I learned a good lesson Saturday. I hope I remember it. I don't want to have to learn it again.

My husband put a screw in the new rake. It won't fall apart. And if I'll just ask, you'll hold me together. Thank you, Father.

## Be

Be...
My Child Be.
In Jesus Christ, In My Spirit,
In My love, My child.
In My light My child.
In My holiness, My child.
In My forgiveness, My child.
In My perfection, My child.
In My Presence. My child.
In My fullness, My child.
In My nature, My child.
In My power, My child.
as
I Am in you,
My child,
Be in Me.

Let me guide you in all you do and in all you say. Be ever mindful of My presence. You have much to offer the kingdom if you let Me have My way. You must be confident in My abilities to produce fruit for My kingdom through you and the gifts I have freely given unto you. You don't have to believe in yourself—believe in Me in you! That's a key to my kingdom. Forget about you—focus on and in Me. I truly have abundant life for you. Just remember Look to Me. Always in every way, remember always in all ways. Believe in Me in you!

# Work Boots Instead of Minks

I smilingly suggested to my husband, just before my birthday, that I thought I was, at my age, ready for a full-length mink coat. He laughed rather uproariously and in between the subsiding laughter he said my present was already bought.

The gift was on the kitchen table when I came home from school. It was wrapped in rather garish Christmas paper, and it was shaped like a shoebox. My husband came down the stairs from his office to welcome me home and present me with my gift.

It was a shoebox and inside was a pair of buckskin ankle high boots. Ankle high boots. The kind my fourth graders, teenagers, and four-year-old grandson wear. He was quite pleased with his purchase. He explained that he knew I had difficulty finding shoes to fit because of my short wide feet—the result of heredity and a childhood of Louisiana barefoot days. He was so pleased with his purchase.

*This is original*, I thought and a long, long way from that mink. But I quickly smiled and thanked him, and I put those work boots on my feet and wore them to dinner with my happy husband. They were comfortable. My toes had room. They weren't all squished up and my feet were warm. The boots were protecting, and they were youth's boots, and I felt young.

In much the same way my husband gifted me with the work boots, instead of the mink, God doesn't always give us exactly what we ask for because we sometimes ask amiss to fill our own lusts.

That's what James tell us. God gives His children what He knows they need. God gives us His work boots, special made to order, just the right size. He clothes the feet of His children in tenacious, durable, rock standing work boots that refuse to allow us to sink in deep mountain crevices. He empowers us with His strength to climb the boulders, to overcome the sharp pointed peaks, to surmount the mountains, to take the toe of our boots in Jesus' name and kick those mountains into that sea Jesus told us about, refusing to have our way blocked to His mountaintop, His Rock. These God shod feet carry us to His place for us in this life.

What a pair of boots! I like my boots...I love my boots! Whose got boots? I've got boots. I'm wearing them to school on Monday. The children will love them.

# No Regrets

It was Thursday evening, and she was tired. She was a teacher in the last week of May—the last week of school. The children were excited about the freedom of summer, their school play, and the end of the year party. They were completely full of themselves. She had final tests to grade, grades to average, report cards to be completed, and a myriad of tasks to complete before her last day of the school year would come. It was the kind of day when she wondered if she were really doing what God had planned for her.

She rarely read the paper. It was always so full of the sadness and the anger of the world. But this evening, wrapped in her old chenille bathrobe and holding a cup of freshly brewed tea, she sat down in the wicker couch near the bay window in her kitchen and, with pen in hand, decided to relax with the daily crossword puzzle. Despite the fact that she avoided the newspaper her husband read from cover to cover, she was an avid reader and once the paper was in her hand, and she was comfortably seated, she began to take in the day's news.

As she read, she came across on article about her own community. Three gardeners were opening their gardens to the public in order to help raise funds for a local endeavor. As she read further, she realized that one of the gardeners was someone she had begun to garden with in her years before she had reentered the teaching profession. As she continued to read about the beauty of the gardens, she thought, "Oh, if I didn't spend so much of my time at school... my flowers would be beautiful too, Lord."

She realized this seemed like such a small matter, but she knew the flowers were only a symptom of a deeper more intimate concern. Was she truly doing what God had called her to do? She reflected on this thought for only a moment when she heard from the Spirit of God to her spirt these words: "The children are your flowers."

God had answered her quiet questions. The tears filled her eyes as she rested in His will for her life. She had no regrets and would have no regrets as long as she continued walking the road He had already carved out for her. She picked up her pen and began working the crossword puzzle, tired, but content.

Seek Me with your whole heart.
Then, You will find Me.
Remember, I told you to slow down,
And live the life I have set before you.
Mercy, My mercy in you.
Hope now in Me.
Have faith in Me.
Remember, let Me be in you!
Let Me do it!

## You've Heard This All Before

I didn't think I'd ever have to say it again, but here I am. Father, forgive me for straying away from you and your Word again.

Why do I quit reading my Bible? I know I have to be fed from your wonderful, delicious, marvelous, loaf of living breathing bread. But somehow, invariably, it happens.

I begin to get a little too sure of myself. I think everything is just going along great, ease up on my Bible study, then the prayer time gets less and less priority. It's not that I don't talk with you. You know I talk with you all day long, and that you are my constant companion.

But I need more of you, don't I, Lord? To keep my mind, body, and spirit holy I must have more of you in my life. You know it, I know it. And precious, precious Father God. I want more of you in my life.

So why am I sitting here having to ask forgiveness again for the same old, same old sin? Because I failed you again. I don't want to fail you. I love you so very, very much. You are my life. You are the best friend I have. You're the greatest listener in the whole universe. You are my buffer from the world. You are my infinite joy. Yet. I stopped reading your Word. God, I'm so grateful that you give me another chance. That you love me enough to have sent my sweet, sweet Jesus to cover my sin of omission. Thank you for your forgiveness...again.

**Our Father who art in heaven hallow it be Thy name
Thy kingdom come...**


If I had my way
If I had my way, there wouldn't be any lonely people in the world
There wouldn't be any pain
There wouldn't be any separation
There wouldn't be any heartache
There wouldn't be any tears of grief
If I had my way
The innocence of childhood would never be taken away
All children everywhere would always, always run and play in joy and walk in
a world filled with peace
No one would ever cry in hunger
No one would lie awake in fear
No one would live in poverty and no one would ever be sick
If I had my way
There would never be another war and disease would not exist
Husbands and wives would be faithful to one another and there would never
be divorce
Families would be close secure and completely loved in a world where there is
no hate
If I had my way
Lord, why do we make it so hard for you?
We who are created in your likeness
You have told us that we are the salt of the earth
The light in darkness
Forgive us for allowing our saltiness to lose its purity
And forgive us, Father, for being so dimly lit
If we would just listen to your words and do your words then, Lord, your way
would be done


**Thy will be done
On Earth as it is in Heaven**

### The Blood-Covered Scar

A wound to the spirit of man runs deep to a place unreachable by the human
hand.
It lies open.
Yet, hidden from human eyes in the inner place.
Red.
Raw.
Oozing tears of inside pain.
Holding feelings inexpressible.
Crying help, me help me God.
Through the darkness of the wound, the blood of Jesus begins to pour.
Washing.
Washing the wounded, lying prostrate at His feet.
His healing hand finds the unreachable place.
The broken spirit of a man.
As the gaping wound receives the blood of Christ, the sacrificial Lamb.
The spirit of man forgives the one who caused his pain.
And in the forgiveness is the healing.
In this forgiveness.
In this healing.
He vows to remember the blood-covered scar left by the wound.
A scar that will help prevent his causing pain to the spirit of any man.
A reminder to walk through the remainder of his life with a compassionate
heart—the heart of Jesus the Christ.
Father, you tell us to do unto others as we would have them do unto us.
Such a gentle tender message.
Such truth.
We ask your forgiveness for hurting one another, Lord.
In Jesus' holy name.

## My Children

You are beginning to understand the depth of my love for my children. I listen to the cries of the afflicted, the lonely, those whose tears won't come. The pain is so deeply intense. Never stop caring for I AM in those who seemingly have stopped—the ones who appear hopeless.

My children are being called to a deeper walk. One of compassion. One of intercession. My eyes are on the righteous and my ears hear their prayers. I have called and called, but few are steadfast and unwavering. My workers must be so diligent, so earnest in seeking my face.

Yes, before you call, I do answer you. But you must be willing to call. I stand at the door of the heart of mankind. Few doors are widely thrown open to receive me. I want to sup with you, to break my bread, and drink my wine with you. I want to make you complete, a new temple. One not made with human hands. I want to decorate you in the oil of gladness. I want the new wine to fill you until you overflow to others. I want to fill you with the peace of God that passes all understanding—My peace. The fruit of the Spirit is within you.

But many of my children only allow me to get a foot in the door of their Spirits. They will not let me in all the way. Don't miss all I have for you. I really did come that you might have life, and that you might have it more abundantly! There are those who are perishing because they don't know My truth. My children must grow up and spread my story. My good news.

My word, it is true. Believe me, abundantly true. YOU are in the world, but be of good cheer, I HAVE overcome the world. Listen to what I say—Open up! Open up! All the way! I knock and knock... reminding you I won't leave you, ever. But there is so much more I have to offer you. All you have to do is believe. Take the time to meditate on my Word and believe me! You are walking in the light!

Now stay in it. The light of the counsel of the Lord Jesus Christ! Live in you! My glory, my joy, my life, my blood, my heart, my child. Open the door all the way...let the Light completely in!

Come up here on this mountain top!
This is where the joy is!
And sing! Sing your songs of joy to me!

## Broken Relationships

We have divided our hearts into separate rooms to which those we care for deeply have individual keys to lock and unlock their rooms at will. These rooms are never the same. Their size depends on the extent of our love for the particular person holding a key, and his love for us. No one can enter or leave a room except the person whose key fits the lock.

If this person ever leaves us or destroys our faith in him, the door to his room will slowly close, for we will try to believe in our friend until the last. But the door does close, and the key does turn in the lock.

Our friend does not return the key, for it is his, and no one can ever take it away from him, not even we ourselves. Even though long years may pass, and many new friends make larger and brighter rooms, that friend who hurt us will still have his room and his key. And though it may never unlock the door again, we know the room is still there.

Father, thank you for the people I have loved, and continue to love even though events and time have taken them out of my life. They are still a part of me. They helped to form the memories of my life. Sometimes those memories are painful, but that's okay. Your Son is the healer of the brokenness in my past. Forgive us our trespasses as we forgive those who trespass against us.

Note: While sitting in the student center at Northeast Louisiana State College, a young man shared the basis of these thoughts with me. From his words came this insight. I don't know his name...but God does.

## Lord, Cleanse Us from All Unrighteousness

Walk through our memories. Help us remember those we have hurt and ask your forgiveness for each one. Help us to remember everyone who has hurt us and give us the nature of Christ so that we will forgive them. We desire to walk in agape love, and oh, dear, dear God. Let it begin in our homes. We ask you to give us the heart of Christ so that His love is completely evident in all who see us. We truly want to walk as a child of the King of Kings and Lord of Lords.

We come against the traditions of man and the traditions of religion that have long held us bound. We bind them in the strong cords of the blood of Jesus Christ and cast them at His feet. In binding these manmade religious traditions in our life, we are free to walk in Your truth and Your light. "What we bind on Earth is bound in heaven, and what we loose on Earth is loosed in heaven." We loose your total truth, freedom and light to us and in us. As members of the body of Christ unify us, Father, in your love.

## I've Done it Again, Lord

Well. I've messed up again—gotten angry over nothing. Why do I let the seemingly small things get to me? What's my excuse? I don't really have a good one, except...it seems to happen when I've just plain overloaded. I know, I know. You've been telling me to rest, but, Lord, how do I do that with 22 ten-year-old children constantly needing attention, and meetings, and carpool duty, recess duty, and lunchroom duty! Father, my job—is it getting harder or is the problem... me?

Anyway, I think I'm sorry for losing my temper, but I'm really not sure. Yes, I am sorry. There's a better way to solve the problem. I did go to the source of problem. That's what you tell me to do. I think we straightened it out. I'm sorry I yelled. I'm sorry I messed up again. Reactive. Reactive. That's what I was today.

You need playtime. I've told you to be as a little child, and children need to play. Take the time to play. This was once your strength. Resurrect your playtime. Regain your joy.

### Girl Child, Girl Child...
### Please Come Out and Play

I was a child for such a very long time.
It seemed to me that life was full of delight and laughter and innocence.
I loved Peter Pan and fell in love with being a child.

I see little girls with pony legs and flowing flying hair, and I wonder... where
the little girl in me has gone and when did the girl child leave?
It seems like only yesterday when my sister and I played on our swing
pretending to be the beautiful ladies on the flying trapeze.

I have grandchildren who call me Grammy.
When did the little girl become the grandmother?
What happened to all the years?

When did I stop chasing fireflies and admiring them captured in my jar?
When did I stop making mudpies and baking them in my backyard?
And when did I stop playing cowboys and Indians and lay my broomstick
horse down?
When did I stop playing Red Light, Green Light and chasing my sister all
around?
When did roly polies stop being so fascinating to me?
When did I stop wading through puddles and running barefoot in the grass?
And when did I stop... stop being a child?

Maybe it was the year my parents died or when the business failed.
Could it have been when my husband thought he didn't really love me
anymore?

I look into the mirror and see the lines, the gray framing my face, and the
glasses adorning my nose.
And this is what I wonder...
Could it be the girl child is only hiding, just waiting to be found?

In the midst of these reflections, I hear my grandson say,
"Come on Grammy, come outside...
Come outside and play with me."

I look down into the laughing eyes of a beloved child seeing me as his friend.

With a small hand clutching mine, and an excited voice saying,
"Let's pretend..."
I enter the world of childhood again.

Girl Child, Girl Child, it's okay to come out and play.
To catch the fireflies, to make the mudpies, to be fascinated by the roly
polies, to ride your stickhorse, and play the children's games.

Hello, Girl Child,
It's so good to have found you again.


Dedicated to Lynn Cross, my dear friend in Christ.
One of God's little children.
(We are all God's little children)

**With Grace**

Lord,
I want to grow older and live every day
of this wonderful life you have given me to the absolute fullest.
The actuality of this older woman I see in the mirror, very often,
and more and more on a regular basis,
overshadows the seventeen year old
I am trying so hard to see there.
And Lord, I'm hearing a whole lot of yes ma'ams and no ma'ams from people
who do not appear to be much younger than me.
Father,
I would really like to do this growing older with grace.


Our Father God
Enjoy this season in your life. Take pleasure in the life I have given
you to live. I chose just the right time for you to be born. I selected your
parents and placed you into the family that would help to form the you of
who you were to become. I have walked beside you every step and heard
every prayer. Yes, you are all grown up now. There has not been a moment of
your life when I have not seen and heard and helped and answered and held
you up and kept you going. Just keep walking...
The journey continues in Me and with Me. This road we walk
together, and you will be seasoned with My grace and grow in My love. The
beauty I see is that of the Spirit and My joy rests within you, and your face
will radiate My life in you. There is no beauty to compare to this. It's going to
be okay; you will do this with grace, My grace. Can you feel my smile upon
you now?

With divine perfect love from my Father God above
the living bread and water you impart
to my ready waiting heart.
I believe...Jesus, I believe your living word.
Jesus, truth your word brings to this child of the King.
As my salvation is ordained and my righteousness is proclaimed,
Faith rises up and sings.
I believe...Jesus, I believe your living word.
Your word lives within me,
Promises of life and health and peace.
Strengthened with your power in this and every eternal hour.
I believe…Jesus, I believe your living word.

# Just a Look

Who was this Zacchaeus? He was a publican, a numbers man, a tax collector. He was not just any tax collector. He was the chief among them. It appears he was the boss tax collector.

Zacchaeus, an intelligent man, used this intelligence in service to the Romans. Thus, he was a wealthy citizen of the town of Jericho.

The people who knew him considered Zacchaeus to be a sinner. Perhaps he was.

A crowd of curious, of scoffers, of believers, of needy hungry people, lined the street on a particular day when Jesus came to town. And this Zacchaeus wanted to see Jesus, to know who He was. He had heard of Jesus. Zacchaeus had been so actively involved with gaining wealth that it would seem he had given Jesus little thought, but maybe he had.

Picture Zacchaeus, head down, as he walked along the street thinking about the tasks set before him when he noticed a large crowd gathering. And Zacchaeus heard someone say, "It's Jesus!" Zacchaeus lifted his head and forgot the business at hand. He thought, "Jesus? I want to see who this man is."

He pushed and shoved trying to get through the crowd. No one gave way to make room for him. He could probably hear them muttering under their breath, "Who does this tax collector think he is? He may be able to tax our goods, but we will give him no place here!"

Being short in stature, Zacchaeus knew he was about to miss seeing this man who proclaimed Himself to be the Messiah. Zacchaeus was a bold Jewish man. He hadn't gained his wealth by being reticent and shy. There was a sycamore tree nearby, and Zacchaeus, quick-witted man that he was, reasoned, "There's a sycamore tree just ahead. I'll climb the tree, then I will see Him." What a great seat Zacchaeus had! Did he care what the people in the crowd thought of him? Probably not.

Because Zacchaeus already knew what the people of Jericho thought of him. Oh, they were nice enough when he came around collecting monies from them. But he was well aware that he was not held in high esteem. If he chose to sit in the tree rather than stretching until his toes hurt, it was his business and his business only. And he really wanted to see this carpenter's son. But it wasn't his business only. It was Jesus's business too. Jesus looked up and said, "Zacchaeus, come down quickly. I need to stay at your house today."

It took just a look from Jesus...There must have been something about the eyes of Jesus, the expression on His face, the acceptance in His voice, for Zacchaeus quickly came down from the tree and, joyfully, he said yes to Jesus.

Zacchaeus and Jesus were the talk of the in crowd. They were whispering behind their hands, "There's Jesus going to eat with another sinner." Did their gossipy attitudes bother the two men? Well, Jesus had heard the words before, and being called a sinner wasn't new to Zacchaeus. No, the words didn't bother them.

Zacchaeus, the tax collector, was so caught up in this encounter with Jesus, with this man who Zacchaeus knew was not just a man, but the Christ, the long awaited Messiah, that he stood and proclaimed to all who would hear, "Lord, I will give half of everything I have to the poor, and if I have taken anything from any man which I shouldn't have, I will repay him four times what I took."

This is a changed man. One look and he grew into a brand new man. I'll give, I'll not take. He is a convert, a believer, a follower of Jesus. Jesus said, "Salvation has come to the house of Zacchaeus. a son of Abraham."

Who was this Zacchaeus? He is our example of a new creature in Christ Jesus. That's how Jesus changes us—in an instant, a new man, a new woman. One encounter with this man Jesus, one look, and we're never the same, never ever the same again.

## A God-Shaped Child

Lord,

I don't want to be a pious self-styled religionist. Deliver me from the Pharisean attitude of self-importance and selfish motivation. Set within me only those attributes, qualities, and gifts that are useful to your service. Provide for me, O God, the creative abilities You need within me to accomplish those things You have given me to do. Set me so firmly on the only Rock and plant me so in Your Word that I grow to the full height and statue You have determined for me to be. Let Your desires become my desires. I want to be what you want me to be, Lord. No more. No less. A God-shaped child...

## And the Walls Tumbled Down

Father, today you showed me that Rahab is in the lineage of Jesus. I've seen this before, but today I learned something. I guess you could say, you talked to my spirit. Rahab, once a harlot, in the lineage of Jesus the Christ. Thank you for choosing her.

Rahab believed in the miracles you performed for your children, and she saw the strength of God in them.

Rahab trusted you, and in this trust, she renounced the city of Jericho and its binding walls of sin in her life.

Rahab placed her life in the hands of your men by hiding Joshua's spies.

Rahab sought and received protection for her entire family.

Rahab obeyed the men of God, and she and her family were delivered.

Rahab became a part of the tribe of Israel.

Rahab married Salmon, an Israelite leader. They had a son. This son, Boar, married Ruth, and the lineage continued to Joseph, the earthly father of Jesus.

Rahab. No one condemned her. You took her into your chosen family, and you continued to bless her—a Godly husband. You looked with such favor on her, an ancestor of Jesus.

Rahab, our example of a woman who believed in the power of almighty God to deliver her and her family. Because of her determination to run away from the old walls of the city that held her captive, you tumbled them down for her and they were never built again.

Thank you, Father, for telling us about Rahab. I really appreciate your sharing your daughter of yesterday with this daughter of today. It's so good to know that it is reality, this acceptance of us as we are. When we trust you, believe you, you deliver us from bondage to the old life. You make us new and then proclaim our righteousness, just as you did for Rahab. Freed from the walls of our past.

## I Am

The world cannot understand that the way to my peace and my restoration is in the will of the Father. The eyes of many leaders are shrouded in darkness. Mankind listens to the wrong voices. The voices of leaders who unknowingly have turned away from my face. They seek the faces of other men, and the advice they receive is the advice of the world.

I Am the answer. If only my children would truly seek my face. Remember, I have told you all the answers are found in me. You must seek me, listen to me, and obey my voice.

Dear Father,

I give you my life so that you will
walk, talk, and love through me.
I am your vessel.
A vessel filled with You!
In Jesus' Name

## But Thomas Didn't Believe...Until...The Touch of Thomas

Thomas was being honest with his fellow disciples and with God. He was grieving for his friend, the Messiah. He didn't understand. He was emotionally wretched and physically spent.

And what did Jesus do for His friend, Thomas? He opened his hands and said, "Touch the wounds, Thomas."

The others had already seen Him, so of course, their faith was certain. But Thomas...God didn't have him with the rest of the disciples when Jesus appeared unto them. I'm glad He didn't. I know Jesus said, "Blessed are those who haven't seen and believe." But isn't it wonderful that God gives us this example of the living breathing Christ loving His friend enough to come to him and proclaim His resurrected power to him?

He didn't condemn Thomas for his open honesty. He didn't shake a finger in his face and threaten him. He didn't make him feel guilty. Jesus simply showed Himself and went so far as to allow Thomas to place his hands on the nail wounds in His body.

Can you picture Thomas doing this? Reaching out, reaching to the openness of Christ, touching the very evidence of Christ's suffering for the salvation of all mankind. Picture the upturned hands of the risen Son of God and the hand of his friend stretched forth to feel the torn flesh of his Lord. Can't you see Thomas' hands shaking as they come in contact with the evidence of the nails and cross? See him tentatively touch the Master...

What must those wounds have felt like to Thomas? The symbols of Jesus' sacrifice and our redemption. He must have felt the compassion, the love, the gentleness, the strength, and the reality of Jesus. Can you see the grief-stricken lined face relax and light up with joy? Can you see defeat turn to victory? Can you see Thomas begin to cry, fall at the feet of Jesus, and say, "My Lord and my Master!" Can you find faith in the touch of Thomas?

Lord, thank you for Thomas and thank you for showing your love and concern for him. I thank you because you understood him, and showed yourself to him, and I know you'll do the same for me.

Yes, Lord, thank you for Thomas.

# And Sarah Laughed

*So, Sarah laughed to herself as she thought, "After I am worn out and my master is old, will I now have this pleasure?" Then the Lord said to Abraham, "Why did Sara laugh and say, 'Will I really have a child, now that I am old?' Is there anything too hard for the Lord? I will return to you at the appointed time next year and Sarah will have a son." Sarah was afraid, so she lied and said, "I did not laugh." But He said, "Yes, you did laugh." Genesis 18: 12-15 NIV*

Sarah laughed, she became afraid, and then she lied, but at the appointed time she gave birth to the promised son, Isaac. She went from laughter, to fear, to lying, to faith in Her Almighty God. She had to come to faith in what God had said He was able to do. Think about it. There was only one man made from the dust of the Earth, Adam. One woman, Eve, made from the rib of man, and there is only one Virgin birth, the birth of our Savior, Jesus the Christ.

Sarah was an old woman. Abraham, an old man. But through faith in the word of God, seed was produced in their bodies. God said, "I will return to you at the appointed time next year, and Sarah will have a son." Nine months, a child is birthed. God was to return the very next year, and Sarah would already have her son. The measure of faith God planted in Sarah began to grow and grow.

Within months the seed of faith had become reality for Sarah and Abraham. Her body had to have taken on newness of life. She had to have come into her menstrual cycle again. Her ovaries began to produce the eggs needed to unite with the sperm of Abraham. God forms us all within our mothers' wombs in the order He has ordained for all mankind.

Isaac was not an exception...

"God calls things that are not as though they were." Sarah had to begin to believe God, and this growing faith in God's word began to abide in her. It grew and grew until her youth was renewed like the eagle's. And Abraham came in unto her and she conceived. As God had promised, "Through faith also Sarah herself received strength to conceive seed, and was delivered of a child when she was past age, because she judged Him faithful who had promised. For God is not a man that he can lie. Every word of God is yea and amen."

Sarah, a mother of God's children because her faith in God's word brought life to her womb. And Sarah became Sarah. Woman of Faith, an example unto us.

## Mary

I love Mary, Mother of Jesus.
She with the mother's heart,
Think of her
Kneeling at the feet of her son,
The tears pouring from her eyes,
drenching the mantle wrapped about her face.
Mary,
Remembering the revelation of the angel telling of the coming of The Son of
God as her own child.
Remembering Joseph with his gentle strength listening to the angel from God
and believing in her innocence and purity.
Mary,
Remembering the stable, the birth of Jesus, and the star leading those God
invited to look upon His Son.
Mary,
Remembering escaping to Egypt and returning home once more.
Watching her son grow as a boy,
Hearing his wisdom,
Seeing his miracles.
Loving him as her Lord and her son, and now,
Reaching with arms upraised,
Longing to hold him just once more.
Hurting with the ache of a mother's grief.
Understanding his sacrifice,
Holding to his promise she would see him again.
Knowing He is God's Son.
Mary,
trusting him.
Completely loving him with a mother's broken heart.
Completely loving him with a believing heart as her Messiah and King.
Mary with the mother's heart woman of faith.

# Easter

We celebrate the joy of new life in the resurrection of the Son of God.
Our Savior,
Jesus the Christ the living Lamb.
We thank God for giving His Son to the world.
This miraculous sacrifice, the light of our spirits.
The day Jesus went to the cross must have been the darkest, yet brightest day
in all of history.
To have borne the sin, diseases, poverties, and weaknesses of all mankind.
Those past, present, future at that blood-stained cross.
He gave His all for the world.
He always knew this was coming,
His perfect bravery.
Love and unselfishness lie open for eyes to see.
Jesus,
How He loves us!
We thank God, that even though we may walk away, the open arms call us
back.
And the cross of Christ releases His blood.
And it drops, covers, renews, saves, and protects us.
That miracle love gift atoning,
Washing,
Cleansing.
How we the children of God give immeasurable thanks for the blessing of
new life.
As the blood of Christ, the very life of Him flows in us and over us.
The protection of the Savior's blood brings resurrection new life.
We ask the forgiveness of our Father God for failing to fathom the depth of
Jesus' love.
As we once again rest in the arms of Jesus the Christ.
May the spiritual eyes of His children be opened by the Holy Spirit to God's
love of humanity.
Through the giving sharing sacrificing of His only begotten Son once for all
mankind.
We thank God there are no more burnt offerings.
Jesus was, is, and always will be the atonement for us.

# The Joy of Christmas

"I give you the joy of Christmas.
The joy that only Christ can bring.
It rings in your heart,
It sings in your heart.
This joy only Christ can bring."

She awakened with these words running through her mind about 3:00 A.M. early in December. Hurriedly, she groped for pencil and paper, scribbled them down, and drifted back to sleep. Later that morning, she read the words again, and realized God had given her a beautiful promise, a gift, one of joy.

Later as she sat in her husband's big comfortable chair, the one she had not wanted him to buy, she pulled the warm old quilt around her and looked into the fire burning so brightly in the fireplace nearby. She leaned back and savored the hot cup of coffee she sipped and enjoyed a moment of calm in the rush of Christmas. She found herself filled with quiet joy, and she began to think of all the beauty found in that three-letter word. Turning the word over and over in her mind and spirit she knew what brought joy into her life.

Joy is knowing she is loved
Joy is peace in her home and in her spirit
Joy is the children coming home
Joy is babies laughing and singing
Joy is drinking a delicious cup of coffee with a dear friend
Joy is getting a letter or telephone call from someone she loves
Joy is being silly and laughing uproariously
Joy is listening to her spirit, being herself
Joy is the sunshine and the bluest of skies
Joy is the spring rains and flowers revealing their glory
Joy is wading in a stream or just sitting on a large rock and watching a trout fisherman artfully cast his line
Joy is the beach at dusk.
Joy is the quiet of snow falling, snow angels, children on sleds and real cooked over the fire hot chocolate
Joy is an old movie, popcorn, a recliner, a fire, and time
Joy is reflection, wonder, and awe
Joy is the fruit of the Holy Spirit living in her
And most of all—Joy is Jesus.

Yes, she knew this would be a special blessed Christmas. The beauty of the infant born two thousand years ago brought true joy into the life He had given her and she thanked God for this holy child Jesus the Christ the greatest of all the Father's gifts. It is in the simple things we find the greatest peace.

## Run Christmas Run

Dear Father,

You know I have not been on my knees or in the Word.
I was so caught up in the everyday events of life. I left you out.
Christmas cards, Christmas money, Christmas gifts.
Christmas parties, Christmas at work.
I know I am responsible for the way I feel today.
I ran and ran.
I don't want to allow this to happen ever again.
Help me schedule the days of my life.
Days filled with your peace and your joy.
I ask your forgiveness for failing you, Father.
I know I have failed you.
Forgive me for getting caught up in the world of materialism again.
Forgive me for worldliness.
I'm so sorry.
Lead me in your Word today.
Put my feet on your path.
You are my God.
Thank you for Jesus Christ, your Son.
Forgive me for treating His birth with negligence this Christmas.
Thank you for His blood that covers all my sins.
Sins removed by His sacrifice on the cross.
Thank you, God for giving me Jesus, and thank you for forgiving me...in Jesus.

## It Doesn't Happen Often Enough

There are lots of things I don't understand, and you want us to understand. Occasionally one of us cares deeply enough and desires your presence in their life so strongly that they sit and sit and sit at your feet. And as they fellowship with you, you share your wisdom with them. You anoint them for a special service to you and your children. It doesn't happen often enough. Does it, Lord?

## God Powered!

When your car is empty of the power of gasoline,
it cannot run. You can fill that tank with water, but the car won't run. In fact,
you have a real problem, if you fill the tank with the wrong liquid.

Now, you can wash your powerless car, wax it, get it looking good,
but it won't get you anywhere. In fact, you'll lose ground.

You put the wrong thing in, wrong things happen to your car.
You have no wheels and loads of repair bills dependent on others to try and
get you around.

Without the Word of God filling us, we would be like the powerless
automobile, looking good on the outside but a real mess on the inside, full of
the ways, desires, and words of the world, stranded and losing ground.

But we put His Word in and take the words of the world out.
We are renewed in His life, running this race He has set before us, mounting
up with wings of eagles with hind's feet for high places. Sounds really good to
me! Instead of the powerless auto, we can be the God powered SSTs!

*In Him was life; and the life was the light of men. John 1:4*

60

Dear Father,

I am so deeply grateful your Word is true.
Your promises are real.
I believe you gave your children the Word as a complete guide.
A guide to a joyful, energetic, faith filled life.
A life of loving, doing, and living to the highest possible degree.
I walk, talk, believe, and do your Word.
Help me to always live continually in the living breathing Word of God.
In Jesus' Name

# The Life Lived in Christ Jesus

*Jesus said, "I am come that they might have life, and that they might have it more abundantly." John 10:10b*

You are the Lord's child, a handmaiden of the Lord, a chosen seed purchased with a price, redeemed, pardoned, set free to walk in victory and freedom, a joint heir with Jesus Christ,
Abraham's seed through the new covenant, washed and purified by the blood of the Lamb, covered in His virtue, blessed of God with unmerited grace and favor, a righteous woman whose steps are measured by God.

You take your place as child of the King. You sit and bathe in the love of Jesus Christ, anointed by the balm of Gilead. The angels of God are your ministering spirits sent forth in Jesus' name to minister to your needs. The Good Shepherd attends to His sheep and knows of your need even before you ask. Therefore, all your wants are satisfied by the Living Word of the Lord. Your heart is fixed on the light, and you are flooded with that light, the love of Jesus Christ. The compassionate heart of Jesus Christ you have been given. You are a servant of the Lord Jesus Christ. He is your strength, and you walk in His revelation knowledge and wisdom for you are of the kingdom of God.

You are the temple of the living God. The Holy Spirit resides within you and fills you with God's power. An intercessor. You present yourself daily to God as a living sacrifice because you trust Him. As He leads step by step, you renew your mind daily in His living breathing word, for it is life to you and health to all your flesh.

Faith fills you through the hearing of God's Word. You keep His word in your ears, your eyes, and in the midst of your heart. You will not be moved. You stand literally on the Word of God. The joy of the Lord is your strength, and your merry heart does you good like medicine. The gladness of God fills you. You taste daily of the Lord, and you always find that He is good. Your Abba Father.

He is I AM that I AM to you. He is all. He sent His word and healed you and delivered you from destruction. He is always holding you in the palm of his hand. He keeps you as the apple of His eye, and He walks beside you, covering you with His wings. He is your refuge and ever-present help. He is the glory and the lifter of your head. His mercy does endure forever.

Therefore, you can do all things through Christ who strengthens you. You wait on the Lord. You walk and do not faint. You run and are not weary. You run the race that is set before you. You have hind's feet for high places. You mount up with wings as an eagle, and your youth is renewed.

You bless the Lord at all times. His praise is continually in your mouth. The Lord is your life, for He does great things always. With the long life you are promised, serve Him joyfully because every day is the day the Lord has made. He called you as an anointed child. He anointed your head. Your cup does run over. His mercy and goodness follow you all the days of your life. He is always before you.

The Lord reigns. Praise the Lord.

Made in the USA
Monee, IL
30 August 2024